# The Pocket Guru

Wow! No-one's got time not to read this!

PEARSON EDUCATION LIMITED
Prentice Hall Business is an imprint of Pearson Education

Edinburgh Gate
Harlow CM20 2JE
Tel: +44 (0)1279 623623
Fax: +44 (0)1279 431059
Website: www.pearson.com/uk

First published in Great Britain in 2011

Pearson Education is not responsible for the content of third-party internet sites.

ISBN: 978-0-273-75519-7

*British Library Cataloguing-in-Publication Data*
A catalogue record for this book is available from the British Library

*Library of Congress Cataloging-in-Publication Data*
A catalog record for this book is available from the Library of Congress

The publisher would like to thank the following for their kind permission to reproduce their images: **Corbis:** pp. 134–5 © Bettmann / CORBIS; **Fotolia.com:** p. 13 © twixx, p. 30 © tdoes, pp. 30–1 © Serhii Novikov, p. 50 © CloverCity, pp. 74–5 © panthesja, pp. 78–9 © ctacik, pp. 94–5 © Maksim Samasiuk, pp. 96–7 © Claudio Baldini, p. 114 © sumnersgraphicsinc, p. 132 © Marc Dietrich, p. 151 © Alexander Raths, pp. 156–7 © shivarider, pp. 162–3 © Elena Schweitzer; **Pearson Education Ltd:** p. 65 © SuperStock. Ingram Publishing. Alamy, p. 104 © Imagestate. John Foxx Collection, pp. 158–9 © Corbis, pp. 168–9 © Comstock Images.

Every effort has been made to trace the copyright holders and we apologise in advance for any unintentional omissions. We would be pleased to insert the appropriate acknowledgement in any subsequent edition of this publication.

10 9 8 7 6 5 4 3 2 1
15 14 13 12 11

Designed by Janet Brown
Typeset in 10/20pt Avenir by Janet Brown
Printed and bound in Great Britain by Scotprint, Haddington, East Lothian

P.S. I've always loved you Alex

Always read the small print

## Dedication

**This book is dedicated to the mini consultants – Ceci, Theo, Archie, Will and Libby.**

## Thanks

We would like to thank the following for their utter helpfulness. Beefing up the content side we've had the input of Lee Kemp, Emma Hendrie, Ralph Browning, Ed McCabe, Dominic Reimbold and Mike Brown. On the design side we've had great technical support from Martin Spear.

We've also had one of the world's finest publishing teams behind us in the form of Rachael Stock, Richard Stagg, Paul East, Nick Gowler and Emma Devlin. We'd also like to thank Rowan Lawton and Juliet Mushens from pfd for their sterling work.

# Contents

**10-POINT PLANS FOR EVERYTHING THAT MATTERS**

# Business Basics

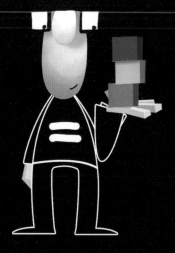

## Create an inspiring strategy

- Decide what you really, really want
- Research. Question. Discuss. Think
- Be crystal clear about the market opportunity
- Think big. Give yourself an epic challenge
- Check where the threats will come from
- Make sure you have the people to deliver
- Work out the first three steps
- Meticulously plan cash in and cash out
- Assume twice as long and double the cost
- Be flexible. Progress is never a straight line

We succeed only when we meet and exceed the expectations of our customers. We have a passion for excellence and endeavour to set and deliver the highest standards of service, value, integrity and fairness. We celebrate the diversity and power of people, ideas and cultures. We respect and enrich the communities in which we do business. We feel a sense of responsibility to lead by example of creativity, enthusiasm and loyalty to our customers.

How to write a
# Mission
# Statement

# Simple Budgeting That Works

(Not for use by top bankers)

- Where is your income coming from?
- When exactly will it hit your account?
- What does each sale cost you?
- What profit do you make on each sale?
- What do your premises cost you?
- What are your staff costs, including you?
- What do you pay for utilities, phones, internet?
- What do travel, advertising and insurance cost?
- How much does your finance cost?
- Profit is what's left when everything else is paid

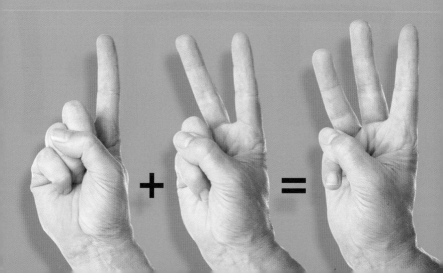

60 Brush

K = 100

7mm

C=16 M=36 Y=36 K=0

Flesh texture
skin 4

# How to Build a Strong Brand

### Define the difference

How does it look different – what's the shape and colour?

How does it sound different – what's the tone of voice?

How does it act differently – what's the personality?

### Protect the difference

Make sure everyone who uses the brand understands it

Have strict brand guidelines – inside the company and out

Be consistent and don't keep changing the brand

### Make the difference

Use the brand in every part of your business

Make your people proud of the brand

Make your customers love every experience of the brand

The Pocket Guru

# This Little Piggy...

## How to master marketing

- Clearly identify your target customers
- Research how they think, feel and buy
- Tell a great story about your product
- Select your media for maximum impact
- Sell emotional benefits, not technical features
- Design everything to be simple and friendly
- Jealously guard the uniqueness of your product
- Make all your communications consistent
- Share the brand vision with all your people
- Create an involved community of customers

# Eat Their Lunch

How to beat the competition

- Know your enemy inside out
- Innovate in the spaces they've left
- Offer a simple alternative to their big product
- Do a better job for one group of their customers
- Create a more attractive brand
- Keep improving customer service
- Be faster and more adaptable
- Build strong partnerships
- Use new channels to market
- Buy them before they get too big

# BUSINESSES ARE BUILT ON
# HAPPY
# CUSTOMERS

- Give them the very best
- Make doing business a pleasure
- Let them choose how to shop
- Bring them fresh, new thinking
- Create a great customer community
- Make paperwork clear and simple
- Act on feedback quickly
- Get their details right
- Keep in contact
- Remember the little touches. They will

# It's a Deal

## Negotiate so you get what you want

- First decide what you'll be happy with
- Be flexible in how you get it
- Know your limits – the red lines
- Remember it's OK to walk away
- Understand what the other guy wants
- Think about how they negotiate
- Generate some options together
- Take your time. There's no rush
- Sort out the little devilish details
- Agree what you've agreed

# ROCK SOLID

Project management

- Plan everything in fine detail
- Check the plans with the delivery team
- Assume plans will have to change
- Build in time and budget contingency
- Give everyone specific tasks
- Build in clear milestones and deliverables
- Hold regular progress meetings
- Flag problems early
- Maintain full and clear records
- Keep customers regularly updated

# Take Your Partners!

## How to work with other businesses

- Get detailed expectations clear at the start
- Understand how your partner works
- Have a clear division of labour
- Put the service agreement in writing
- Plan your work together well in advance
- Be fair with time and money
- Let your people talk to their people
- Give regular, honest feedback
- Build in regular reviews and exit points
- Help them grow their business

- Only meet if you really need to
- Plan exactly what you want to achieve
- Invite only useful, interested people
- Let people know why you're meeting
- Make sure everyone knows each other
- Control airtime. Hear from everyone
- Beware of agenda hijackers. Stay focused
- Finish before people mentally leave
- Agree who does what when
- Follow up individually. You'll learn stuff

# Beautiful Meetings

Ones that are worth having

# Smooth
# Operations

# Off Colour?

## Business healthcheck

| | | | |
|---|---|---|---|
| **Products** | Attractive | Functional | Reliable |
| **Logistics** | Fast | Flexible | Efficient |
| **Technology** | Responsive | Enabling | Robust |
| **Innovation** | Products | Services | Markets |
| **Accounts** | Accurate | Helpful | Timely |
| **Customers** | Loves | Hates | Wants |
| **Service** | Simple | Friendly | Trusted |
| **Communication** | Staff | Customers | Partners |
| **People** | Trained | Focused | Motivated |
| **Ethics** | People | Environment | Community |

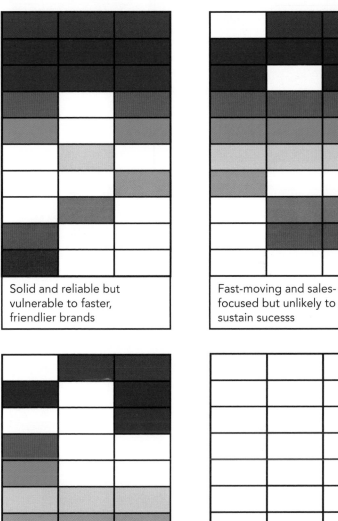

Solid and reliable but vulnerable to faster, friendlier brands

Fast-moving and sales-focused but unlikely to sustain sucesss

People-focused but not enough technical and process innovation

# RETHINK

## Shortcuts to innovation

- Import good ideas to your business
- Export your good ideas to other markets
- Redesign things to look or feel better
- Make it disposable or longer lasting
- Make it more exclusive or cheap and cheerful
- Cut out the middleman and do it direct
- Become the middleman and add value
- Make a small thing bigger or a big thing smaller
- Make a difficult thing easier
- Start with a new brand and a new story

# PRODUCTIVITY BOOSTERS
## Get more out of your existing business

- ○ Measure everything you do already
- ○ Have clear objectives for improvement
- ○ Get the team leaders motivated
- ○ Ask your front line for ideas
- ○ Introduce flexi-time for your people
- ○ Degunge all processes
- ○ Only deliver what the customer wants
- ○ Streamline your support functions
- ○ See what else your technology can do
- ○ Pay on performance

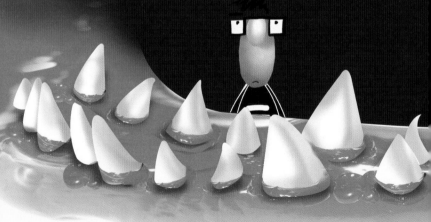

# RISK

Sensible precautions to
stop bad things happening

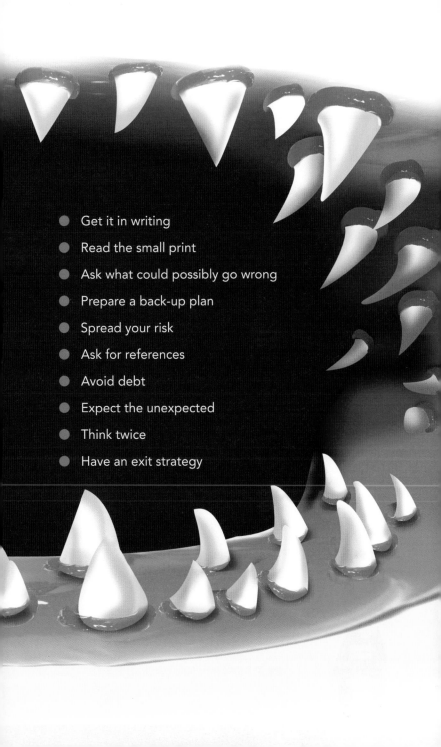

- Get it in writing
- Read the small print
- Ask what could possibly go wrong
- Prepare a back-up plan
- Spread your risk
- Ask for references
- Avoid debt
- Expect the unexpected
- Think twice
- Have an exit strategy

# Think of a
# Number

## How to prepare a sales plan

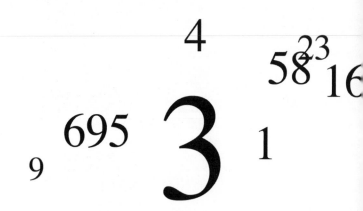

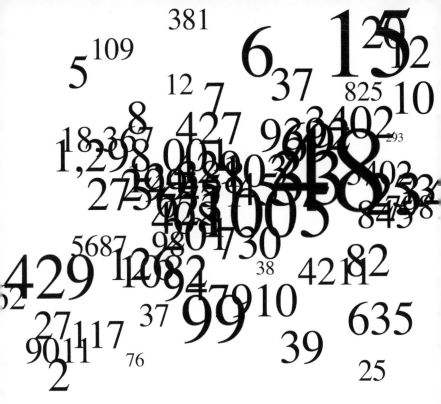

- What new customers are you targeting?
- What's an achievable conversion rate?
- What repeat business can you expect?
- List short and long-term objectives
- Make them specific, measurable, ambitious
- Divide objectives into actions
- Break down by geography, accounts or sectors
- Prioritise prospects for sales potential
- Allocate resources to priorities
- Draw up an action plan with calendar

# Air
# Head

## How to survive business travel

- Think every stage through before you go
- Put vital documents online for retrieval
- Only take hand luggage and keep it close
- Photocopy vital travel documents
- Pack plugs for phones, ears and baths
- Confirm travel, meetings and contacts
- Take small change and a large credit card
- Dress for local climate and customs
- See the sights – you may never return
- Always take a good book. It works anywhere

# Bigger Bottom Lines

## How to increase profit

- Sell more
- Increase your prices
- Reduce the cost of labour
- Boost your productivity
- Identify and reduce waste

- Squeeze suppliers

- Renegotiate raw materials

- Find new places to distribute products

- Spend less on expensive professional services

- Sharpen the targeting of your marketing expenditure

# The Heart of the Customer

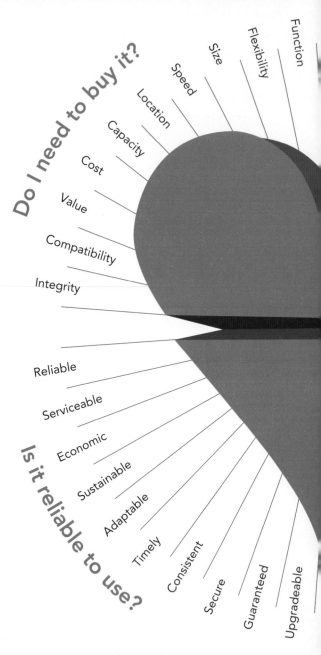

# What makes it tick

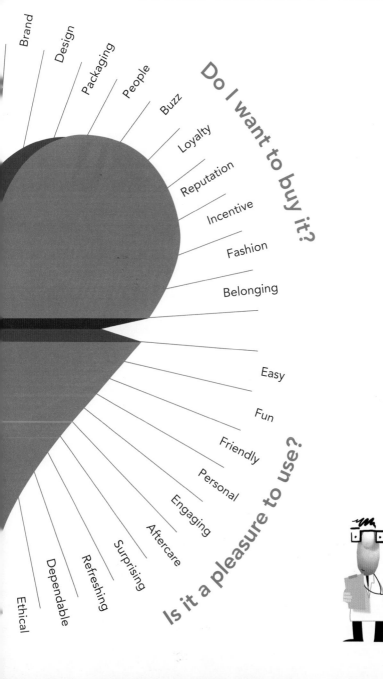

Brand
Design
Packaging
People
Buzz
Loyalty
Reputation
Incentive
Fashion
Belonging

Do I want to buy it?

Easy
Fun
Friendly
Personal
Engaging
Aftercare
Surprising
Refreshing
Dependable
Ethical

Is it a pleasure to use?

# What Crisis?

Managing bad things so well
they almost look good

- Get the facts and face them
- Realise it's not the end of the world
- Take responsibility and then act
- Stop the bleeding
- Find the root of the problem
- Focus everything on recovery
- Think hard, fast and creatively
- Say sorry – and mean it
- Try to make amends
- Make sure you learn the lessons

# Up the Creek

## Managing cash flow to pay the bills

- Work out when you need to pay and be paid
- Remember it's not a sale until you're paid
- Start chasing payment early
- Offer incentives for early payment
- If you can, hold something back until payment
- Prioritise payments. Who must be paid now?
- Keep your creditors informed
- Be very clear about your payment terms
- Know your legal rights
- Be nice. Be polite. Be tough. It's your money

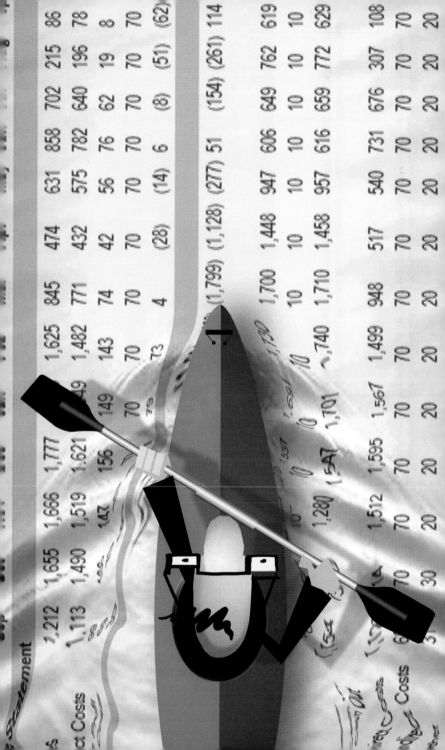

# Pitch
## Perfect

How to win a contract

- Earn a place on the pitch list

- Ask detailed questions about the brief

- Understand how they purchase

- Know what the competition offers

- Take time to really think about the problem

- Answer the brief in a fresh way

- Make your presentation beautiful

- Coach your references how to sell you

- Stay well ahead of deadlines

- Justify your costs and sell your value

# You've Done the Work, Now Get Paid

Get payment terms in writing – 30 days!

Send your invoice pronto, while your work's still piping hot

Address your invoice to a real person with a real phone number

Payments often happen once a month – don't miss it

Call accounts the day after your payment is due – surprise them!

Always be polite to people in accounts – they're human too.

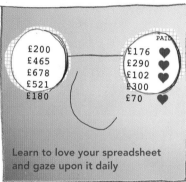

| | PAID |
|---|---|
| £200 | £176 ♥ |
| £465 | £290 ♥ |
| £678 | £102 ♥ |
| £521 | £300 ♥ |
| £180 | £70 ♥ |

Learn to love your spreadsheet and gaze upon it daily

Ask bad payers to pay upfront – upset them before they upset you

Chase bad debtors hard – they'll eventually pay for peace and quiet

HELP

If you don't like doing it, get someone else to manage your invoices

# Personal Training

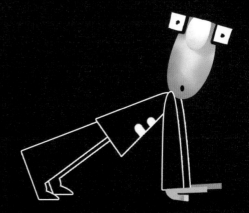

# WORK

How to do stuff you hate

# PAIN RELIEF

- Make it the first thing you do
- Remind yourself of the benefits
- Talk to people. Reduce the fear
- Ask for support
- Plan in detail
- Commit to a start time
- Make the first step the easiest
- Remember it could be a lot worse
- Plan a reward for yourself
- Start now. Get it over with

# Magic Pants

## Stay in control without being a freak

- Be clear about your own agenda
- Allow yourself time to think
- Keep on top of your inbox
- Plan ahead. It's later than you think
- Work out what makes other people tick
- Be flexible in your approach
- Take time before responding
- Check in with people regularly
- Keep on top of the finances
- Prepare for the best and the worst

Nice Guys Finish
# Happiest

Personal values that work at work

- ◯ Listen to people
- ◯ Be generous with your talents
- ◯ Don't speak ill of the living
- ◯ Hurting other people hurts you more
- ◯ Take time to say thank you
- ◯ If it feels wrong, it is wrong
- ◯ Don't discriminate against humans
- ◯ Volunteer to make things better
- ◯ Give as much as you take
- ◯ Keep your desk and conscience clear

# Relax...

Manage stress before you can't manage anything else

- Be clear what you do and don't want
- Say thank you, but no thank you
- If it's not necessary, don't do it
- Simplify everything you do
- Plan relaxation time
- Relax your body and your mind will follow
- Laugh, eat lunch, have a chat
- Good communication always helps
- Never take your work home
- Relax, it's only a job

# About Time!

Time is money. Spend it wisely

- Don't accept impossible deadlines
- Negotiate schedules
- Promise it later, deliver it earlier
- Time spent planning always saves time later
- Build in contingency time. You'll need it
- Communicate progress regularly
- Allow time for checking stuff
- Everything has a cycle. Go with it
- Don't give time to time wasters
- Start work now. It's later than you think

# Squeeze Your Creative Juices!

## Give your brain its head

- Put what you know aside for a moment
- Think about something completely different
- Imagine how things could be
- Know the golden rules, then break them
- Draw your problem and then redraw it
- Find new words for new ideas
- Try varying time, money and people
- Import an old idea into a new place
- Solve the problem behind the problem
- Liberate the simple from the complex

# Thank God it's
# Monday!
## How to go to work happy

- Do something worth doing
- Work an eight-hour day
- Be relaxed about stress
- Work with people you like
- Help others enjoy their work
- Take pride in what you do
- Walk, run or cycle to work
- Learn something new every day
- Do more of what you're good at
- Avoid vending machines

# Butterflies?

## Confidence tricks for caterpillars

- What exactly scares you? Really?
- Talk through your fears – it shrinks them
- Remember no-one else is perfect
- Say hello quickly. The rest is easy
- Smile – it kick-starts confidence
- Go at your own pace
- Don't talk yourself down
- Focus on your strengths
- Do your best, then relax
- Be yourself – it's what you're best at

# How to make Big Decisions

you won't bitterly regret for years afterwards

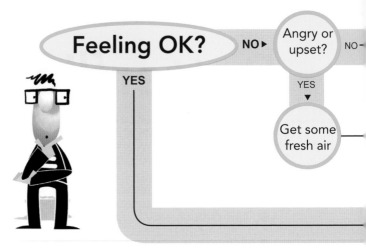

**Feeling OK?** NO ▸ Angry or upset? NO–

YES

YES

▼

Get some fresh air

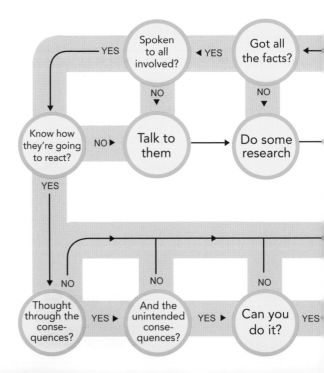

Spoken to all involved? ◂ YES Got all the facts? ◂

YES

NO ▼ NO ▼

Know how they're going to react? NO ▸ Talk to them → Do some research →

YES

▼

NO — NO — NO

Thought through the conse-quences? YES ▸ And the unintended conse-quences? YES ▸ Can you do it? YES

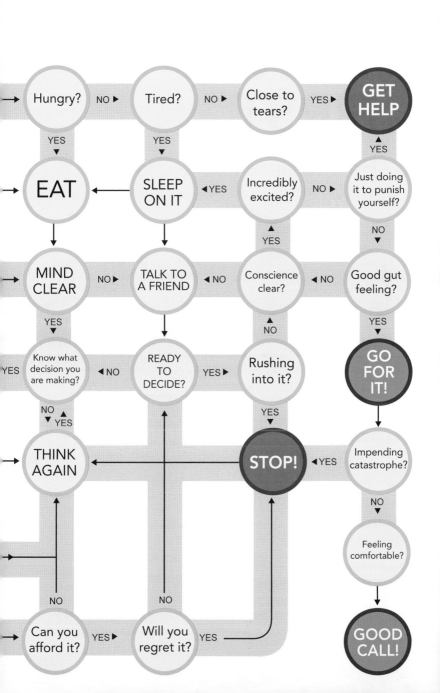

# FIRST
# THINGS
# FIRST

## How to prioritise

1. Urgent, important and interesting

2. Urgent, important but not interesting

3. Important, interesting but not urgent

4. Urgent, interesting but not important

5. Important but not interesting or urgent

6. Urgent but not interesting or important

7. Interesting but not urgent or important

8. Not urgent, important or interesting

Listen

Make time

Empathise

Remember names

Say thank you

Celebrate success

Notice small things

Keep in touch

Look for the best

Make coffee

Be polite

Relax

Don't whinge

Be optimistic

Give good feedback

Admit to mistakes

Ask questions

Wash

Resolve conflict

Inspire

Lead by example

# Interpersonal Skills

Don't judge

Include people

Say hello

Pay your debts

Love your family

Control your ego

Help out

Wait your turn

Have a laugh

Introduce people

Be on time

Forgive

Smile

Be interested

Respect differences

Trust people

Keep an open mind

Be patient

Stay calm

Gather opinions

Go for lunch

# Work
# Fitness

## How to keep fit in the office

- Sit up straight. Give your lungs a chance

- If it's less than 20 floors, use the stairs

- Do something active in your lunch break

- Bring your own lunch. It's cheaper and healthier

- Put a bottle of water on your desk and finish it

- Fill your drawer with fruit and nuts

- Walk to the furthest bathroom in the building

- Try walking, cycling or canoeing to work

- Give yourself thinking time in the gym

- Do butt squeezes (your own) in meetings

| | | | | |
|---|---|---|---|---|
| Jump in | Choose | Harmonise | Check timing | Persuade |
| Distribute | Follow orders | Mutiny | Rise above it | Panic |
| Consult widely | Control | Leave | Accept | Reject |
| Redesign | Laugh it off | Negotiate | Debate | Find |
| Delay | Compromise | Imagine | Argue | Listen |
| Respond | Correct | Delegate | Act calmly | Wait |
| Speed up | Repeat | Move | Emphasise | Rethink |
| Go back to basics | Confront | Invest | Rest | Pay |
| Clarify | Promise | Get it in writing | Stop | Go for a walk |
| Meet up | Apologise | Learn | Improve | Let off steam |

| Build on it | Say thanks | Dream | Buy | Fight back |
|---|---|---|---|---|
| Step back | Change | Simplify | Search the net | Disagree |
| Plan | Brainstorm | Sell | Ignore | Slow down |
| Look into | Pray | Support | Research | Offer help |
| Reconcile | Seek assistance | Redefine | Acknowledge | Develop |
| Relax | Champion | Agree | Sleep on it | Celebrate |
| Embrace | Park | Take legal advice | Divide up | Avoid |
| Publicise | Communicate | Start again | Say nothing | Look up |
| Review | Appeal | Think | Reward | Travel |
| Follow instinct | Explore | Go home | Prioritise | Check facts |

# Managing People

# FOLLOW ME FOLLOW

## Natural leadership

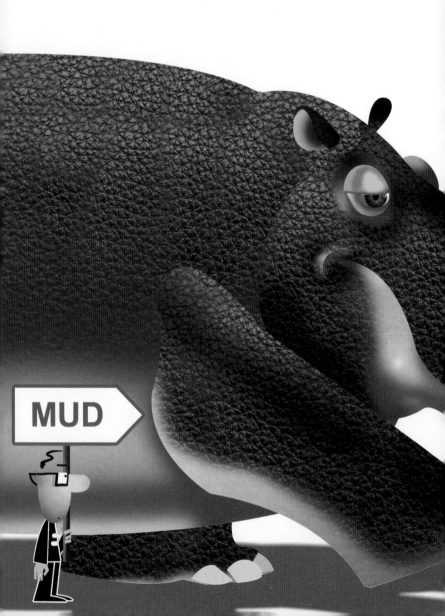

- Passionately believe in your vision
- Build a team that shares your vision
- Work harder than anybody else
- Keep your problems to yourself
- Tell your team exactly what you expect of them
- Listen to your team and respect their skills
- Keep everyone informed and motivated
- Give clear orders and make sure they happen
- Very occasionally be ruthless
- Share the profits

# Change People

## So they hardly know you're doing it

- You can't force change – make people want it
- Get them on your side by listening first
- Understand why they do what they do
- Assume they want the best outcome
- Show why their good intentions go wrong
- Ask what small change would get better results
- Make sure the change makes them look good
- Show what a fantastic difference the change makes
- Keep an eye on things – don't let them slip back
- Never underestimate laziness, incompetence and fear

# Hold Me Back!

How to keep people motivated

- Be motivated yourself – it's infectious
- Find out what fires people up
- Set them an interesting challenge
- Treat people with respect
- Listen to them
- Let them do it their way
- Allow them to fail and learn
- Stick up for them
- Reward achievement
- Promote talent

# Look at You!

## Giving a good appraisal

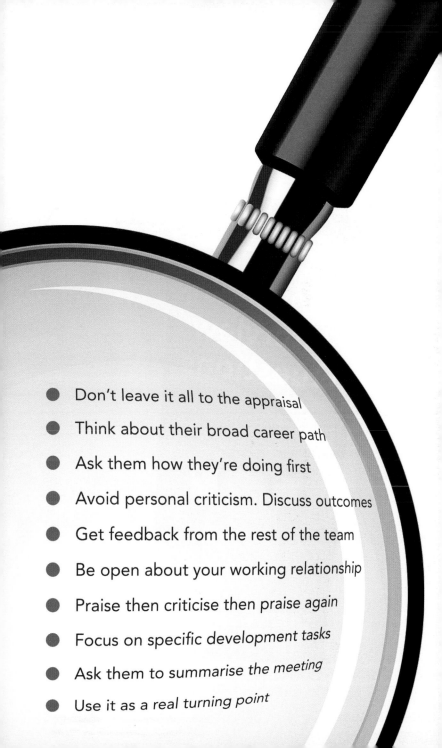

- Don't leave it all to the appraisal
- Think about their broad career path
- Ask them how they're doing first
- Avoid personal criticism. Discuss outcomes
- Get feedback from the rest of the team
- Be open about your working relationship
- Praise then criticise then praise again
- Focus on specific development tasks
- Ask them to summarise the meeting
- Use it as a real turning point

- Tell us about yourself
- Why do you want to work here?
- What did you learn in your last job?
- If you got this job, what would you do with it?
- What one thing about yourself would you fix?
- How do you work with other people?
- What are your first impressions of us?
- Where do you want to be in 10 years' time?
- What one thing are you proud of?
- What haven't we covered?

# BAST

## How to manage them

- Ideally avoid them
- Don't threaten them
- Get to know their boss
- Make your work above reproach
- Stay calm always
- Get what they say in writing
- Manage them proactively
- Develop a support network
- Anticipate trouble
- Attack only with overwhelming force

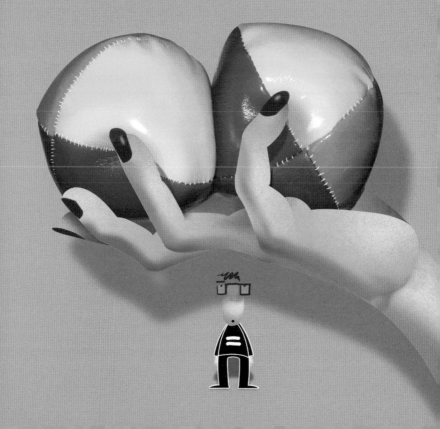

# Workingwith
# Genius

Managing people who think they are one

- Be relaxed about different behaviours
- Help them focus their genius
- Give them really challenging problems
- Encourage a continual flow of ideas
- Protect creatives from bureaucracy
- Introduce subtle competition
- Keep them stimulated (with stimuli)
- Allow ideas time and space to develop
- Team creatives up with implementers
- Reward people for thinking differently

# Fly Me to the Moon!

How to set crunchy **goals**

- Describe in detail the desired outcome
- Explain why it's worth having
- Have a way of measuring the goal
- Make sure the goals are completely agreed
- Goals should be attainable but ambitious
- There should be an agreed timescale
- Assess support needed to achieve goals
- Be prepared to change the goals over time
- Arrange regular progress reports
- Get people to grow their own future goals

# Coaching

Helping people to help themselves

- Set aside quality time for regular meetings
- Remember it's a joint approach
- Make sure you understand what they do
- Agree what changes you both want to see
- Be continually supportive and suspend judgement
- Listen and ask questions to get more context
- Help people to think for themselves
- Resist the urge to suggest solutions
- Set realistic goals and milestones together
- Check in regularly to monitor progress

# It's Great Here!

How to have a happy office

- Pay a decent wage
- Solve process nightmares
- Have approachable leaders
- Let people work flexi-time
- Communicate well at all levels
- Get rid of status symbols
- Reward and recognise effort
- Make meetings quick and useful
- Don't over-organise 'fun'
- Lay on a good canteen

# YOU ARE IN MY
# POWER

Getting people to want what you want

- Be clear what you want

- Want it passionately. Enthusiasm sells

- Get all the facts, including the unhelpful ones

- Engage with people before you need to

- Never assume others assume what you assume

- Highlight for others the benefits of your way

- Warn of the dangers of other routes

- Acknowledge people's feelings. Go with them

- Make your idea seem the natural endpoint

- Be polite, persistent and persuasive

# Office Politics

## How to tread carefully

- Be transparent in all your actions
- Communicate with all sides
- Have allies in all departments
- Identify and watch the politicians
- Understand what threatens them
- Get important things in writing
- Have friends in high places
- Be clearly good at your job
- Talk with before you're talked about
- Assume the best in people. Once

# Hair down!

# Celebrating success

- Mark success with an event
- Tell everyone why their part was vital
- Talk through what went right
- Get a good photo of the team
- Promote people while they're confident
- Publicise success internally and externally
- Get a thank you from the big boss
- If you've worked hard, give people time off
- Remember cash is always welcome
- Look forward to the next success

# The Ropes

## How to run inductions

- Make contact before new people start
- Try to do inductions in groups
- Avoid videos. Hairstyles change
- Show them to as many people as possible
- Walk them round the whole site
- Tell them what's expected of them
- Make sure they've got all their kit
- Give everyone a buddy
- Have a follow-up meeting after a month
- Ask them for their first impressions

# Communication

# THICK HEADS

## Get stuff in there by communicating better

- Be clear about the change you want
- If you really believe it, show it
- Listen before you think before you speak
- Headlines first, then the whole story
- Consistency is the clearest message
- If it really matters, do it face to face
- Involvement is the best persuader
- Encourage feedback and act on it
- Little and often is better than long and loud
- You've been heard when things change

# Inbox Invaders
## Winning the email battle

- If it really matters, talk to people
- Rediscover the power of the telephone
- Handwritten letters don't get deleted
- Don't email people visible from your desk
- If you don't send, they won't reply
- Get yourself off distribution lists
- Don't send or forward junk
- If you open it, deal with it
- Remember no-one reads more than six lines
- Emails biodegrade if left long enough

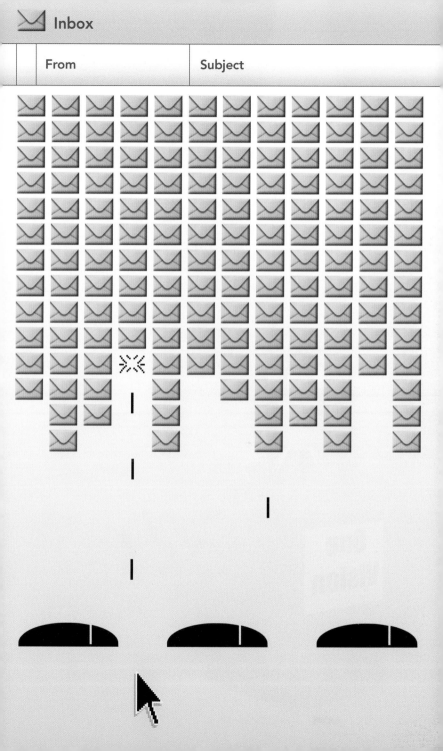

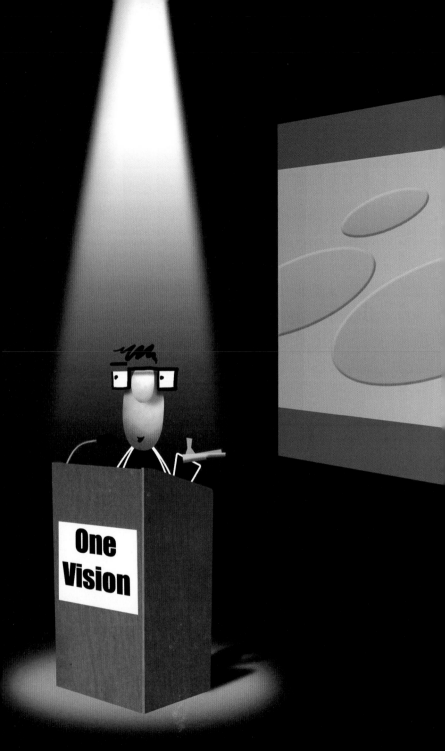

- Have a clear purpose
- Plan well ahead
- Hold the event somewhere fresh
- Have one person in charge
- Don't attempt too much
- Make sure the 'fun' is actually fun
- Interaction creates energy
- Boring presenters drain energy
- Good food always helps
- Get expert technical help

# Meetings of Minds

How to run a brilliant event

# BAM

## How to write well in business

Starting with a bang grabs your readers. Keep them interested by promising them something good...

After you've read this you'll never write the same way again (get the word 'you' in quickly to show it's all about them).

My friend Alicia used to write the world's dullest email. Not any more! She keeps her sentences short and sweet. Like this one. She now writes more like she talks. It's more natural and keeps you interested.

We don't know who this Alicia is but we like her. That's how good examples work. Use them often.

Choose your words as if picking the first chocolate from a box. There are plenty of delicious, nuggety ones to choose.

Before you print or send, read it froo. You'll pick up embarrassing mistakes like 'froo'.

Get rid of any repetition or over-explanation. Then get rid of any repetition or over-explanation.

Have a beginning where you hook them, a middle where you reel them in and an end that lands them where you want them.

It's persuasion on paper!

# A4

## How to fit your thoughts on one side

210

297

# HOW TO GET YOUR MESSAGE ON ONE SIDE OF A4

## Introduce the subject

Business people are hungry for information but don't have much time to consume it. Give someone a fat report and they'll look at the executive summary at the beginning and the costs at the back.

## Give your opinion

The secret of effective business communication is brevity, clarity and good organisation. We all need to be able to give the maximum possible information in the clearest and shortest way.

## Support your argument

### 1. Brevity

Decide what your most important message is and stick to it. Keep your supporting facts and figures separate – if people want them they can find them but they shouldn't get in the way.

### 2. Organisation

Organise your material the way it's set out on this page:

- Start with the background, context or brief. This focuses the reader
- Say what you think – this is the bit that really counts
- List supporting points – include opposing views and deal with them
- Conclude by repeating your main argument and listing actions

### 3. Clarity

It's best to be single-minded. You can't say everything but make sure you say something. Don't use the passive. Be positive: 'I believe' or 'I recommend'. Take responsibility so you can take the credit later.

A good way of being clear is OPINION + FACT + REASON + EXAMPLE

I believe we should eat more fruit. Fruit is vital to a balanced diet. It's full of minerals and vitamins. One orange gives you all your daily requirement of Vitamin C.

## So what now?

Business communication should be short, clear and well organised. We now need to:

1. Take a copy of this
2. Use it as a guide in our writing
3. Study the structure of other communications
4. Only use one side of A4 whenever possible

How to give someone

# A Damn
# Good
# Listening To

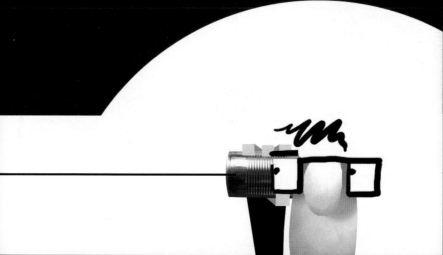

# New & Improved

## How to get impressive training results

- Clearly sell the benefit of training
- Know your subject inside out
- Do a live trial and learn from it
- Have plenty of useful, meaty content
- Let people interact and get involved
- Provide useful notes in a usable format
- Keep groups small and mix them up
- Get commitment to use the learning
- Check what was useful
- Keep refreshing your training

# THAT RINGS A BELL

## A BELL

### REDISCOVER THE LOST ART
### OF THE TELEPHONE

- Plan what you need to talk about
- Give it 100% concentration
- Check that it's a good time to talk
- Start with some general chit-chat
- Talk in short bursts and check they're with you
- Don't take other calls. Everyone hates it
- Say yes regularly. It's verbal nodding
- Finish by repeating what you've agreed
- Follow up immediately before you forget
- Sometimes call when you don't need to

# Now
# You're
# Talking

Speeches to make
people sit up and listen

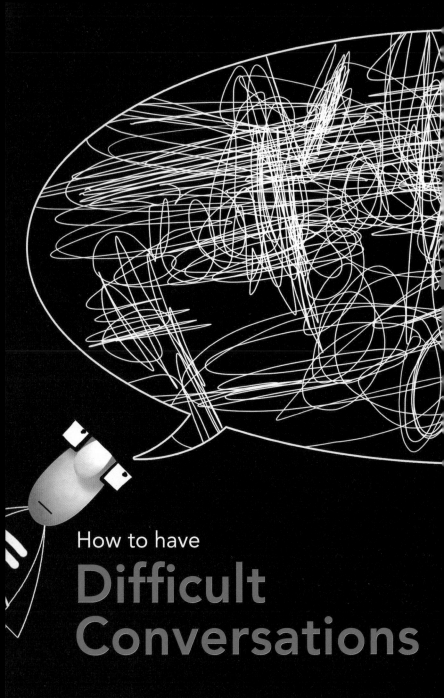

How to have
Difficult
Conversations

- Choose your time carefully
- Allow plenty of time
- Be crystal clear what you need to get over
- State your position calmly
- Understand where they're coming from
- Hear them out and clarify points
- Acknowledge feelings on both sides
- Closely define where you disagree
- Brainstorm options to close the gap
- Commit to a plan before you finish

# Team Briefings

## Keeping them short and sweet

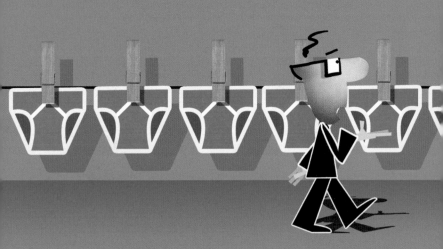

- Establish a regular time and place
- Create an informal atmosphere
- Review progress since the last meeting
- Give the facts quickly and clearly
- Include everybody in the discussion
- Take feedback and act on it
- Be aware of how the team is feeling
- End with agreement on the way forward
- Commit to timed, measurable actions
- Allow time for reward and recognition

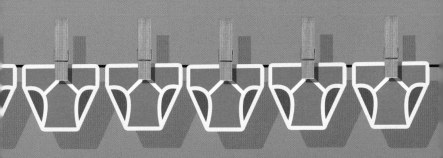

# Getting Ahead

# UP

## How to move in that direction

- Concentrate on what you do best
- Be enthusiastic – it's contagious
- Talk to people with experience
- Take short-term pain for long-term gain
- Under-promise and over-deliver
- When you're ready, take the big risk
- Time wasters shorten life. Avoid them
- The harder you fall, the harder you become
- No is a diversion, not a stop sign
- Keep looking upwards and outwards

# Who is that
## Wonderful
# Person?

How to get noticed at work

- Say hello. Get people to know you
- Make friends in other departments
- Volunteer for projects
- Have good ideas and take the credit
- Talk to senior management
- Organise social events
- Work fast and help other people
- Write for the office paper or blog
- When your boss does well, tell them
- Visit HR. They know stuff

# Money

## How to make more

- Focus your efforts
- Improve skills that are valuable
- Ask for more money. Shyness is expensive
- Cut costs that aren't useful or enjoyable
- Always get a better quote
- Get performance-related pay and then perform
- For a big salary rise, change company
- For really big money, own the company
- Become an expert in one thing
- Look after the pounds and forget the pennies

# Bull Riding

## How to manage your boss

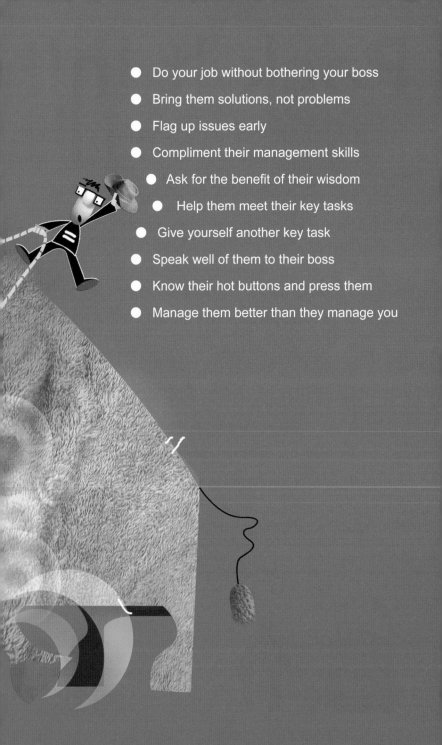

- Do your job without bothering your boss
- Bring them solutions, not problems
- Flag up issues early
- Compliment their management skills
- Ask for the benefit of their wisdom
- Help them meet their key tasks
- Give yourself another key task
- Speak well of them to their boss
- Know their hot buttons and press them
- Manage them better than they manage you

# Pack It In!!

## Get more done by working smarter

- Organise your brain before your technology
- Work an hour before or after everyone else
- Think in the morning, do after lunch
- Work in small, digestible chunks
- If you're not adding value, delegate
- Write your agenda and stick to it
- Put time for communication in the diary
- Be very selective about meetings
- Keep your desk and inbox clear
- Plan for tomorrow but act today

FRANK          FRANK

# Frank
# Exchange

Good appraisals with your boss

- Decide what you need to get out of the appraisal
- Try to anticipate what might come up
- Talk about your issues and aspirations
- If you feel it strongly, say it clearly
- Don't be defensive – use criticism constructively
- Remember that everything is negotiable
- Get feedback and goals in writing
- Ask for extra training and support
- Take away the good stuff as well as the bad
- Think positive and try to enjoy it

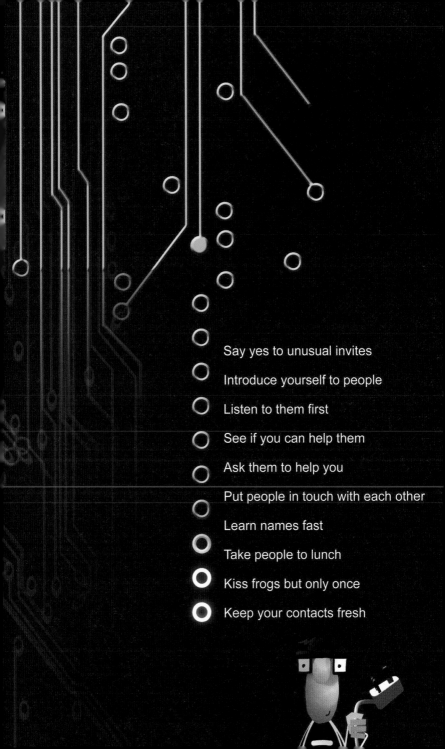

Say yes to unusual invites

Introduce yourself to people

Listen to them first

See if you can help them

Ask them to help you

Put people in touch with each other

Learn names fast

Take people to lunch

Kiss frogs but only once

Keep your contacts fresh

# Board
# Surfing

## How to survive on the Board

- Do the spadework before the meeting
- Tell the Chair what's on your agenda
- Remember the Board is expected to lead
- Beware of factions and politics
- Understand and use personal agendas
- Make sure you're on top of the numbers
- Keep in touch with the front line
- Avoid murky skullduggery
- Delegate detailed work to sub-committees
- Bring the rest of the business with you

Playa Del Excito
Costa De Riquesas
Las Islas Tranquillas
Eldorado

MADE
IT!

HOW TO MANAGE SUCCESS

# POSTCARD

AIR MAIL

- Take time to enjoy your success
- Understand how you made it
- Look out for new threats
- Understand what success buys you
- Plan your succession
- Help other people to succeed
- Get the paperwork straight
- Share the fruits with all who grew it
- Mend the roof while the sun shines
- Now learn something new

# Moving On

# Burnt Fingers

How to start again, stronger and wiser

- Face the facts

- Make sure you've learned the lessons

- Don't waste energy on revenge

- Keep hold of the people you value

- Sort out your personal life

- Take a break and recoup your energy

- Listen to your instincts about what's next

- Go and talk to interesting people

- Be open to completely new things

- Don't forget your dreams

# Write a

# Good

# CV

# John Appleseed *Bigger font*

12 Braeburn Way, Dengling, Somerset, TN1 8JB          Date of Birth: 1 April 1985
Phone: 01234 5678          Mobile: 07777 777777          Nationality: British
Email: j.appleseed@goldendelicious.net

*All vital!*

---

## Personal profile *Don't be shy, tell them why you're good!*
- Skilled apple picker, orchard manager and gang leader
- Experience with other fruit – pears, quince, oranges, lemons
- Friendly, self-motivating manager with excellent interpersonal skills

## What I'm looking for next in my career *Make sure this fits the job you're applying for*
- Senior orchard manager
- Larger operations
- More involvement in commercial operations

---

## Work experience *Plenty of detail here*
Head picker Cowley Orchard          April 2008 – September 2011

Co-ordinated three gangs over five orchards for average of 10K seasonal tonnage

Assistant head picker Cowley Orchard          November 2004 – April 2008
Assisted with co-ordination of gangs and was leader of apple gang of 30 pickers

*Keep it relevant*
Farm labourer Somerset          October 2003 – November 2004
General farm labouring including tree planting, pruning and husbandry

Volunteer lemon picking in Spain          June – September 2003
Worked with international gangs. Promoted gang leader

---

## Relevant skills
Languages: Fluent in Spanish and a little Mandarin          Driving licence: Full clean
Computer skills: Familiar with all Apple Macs. Especially Dual Core processors
Education: *If you've got an MBA don't worry about GCSEs*
- BA Newcastle University – Agricultural Sciences
- PhD Oxford University – Apples and their contribution to gravitational theory
- Harvard University – Masters in the Business of Apples

### Activities and interests
- Cider drinking
- National Crumble Making Champion 2006
- Apple bobbing
- ~~Naked mud wrestling~~          *Make sure they're interesting and don't include anything too controversial*

---

## References *Check with them first*
Grannie Smith   12 Acacia Gardens, Roxburgh
Rosie Pippin    Old Acre Farm, Westingbourne, Somerset

# Adiós Amigos!!

How to leave a job properly

- Never quit in a hissy fit
- Plan your exit before you resign
- When you're calm, make the decision
- If it feels right at 9am, it probably is
- Carry on working happily
- Quietly look for a better job
- Don't leave until you've got one
- Be nice. You may meet again
- Help manage the handover
- Take time to breathe between jobs

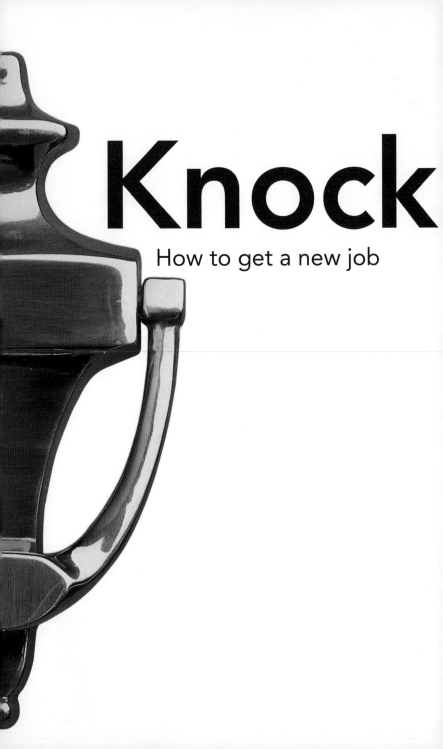

# Knock

How to get a new job

# Knock

- Decide you want a new job
- Ask HR for a new one
- Rebuild your existing job
- Upgrade your CV
- Upgrade your expectations
- See what's out there
- Talk to headhunters
- Raise your profile in the industry
- Talk to people with an open mind
- Take big risks in your current job

# In the Hot Seat
## Staying cool in job interviews

- Do your research. It's all on the internet
- Think what they're likely to ask
- Be on time, look smart, relax
- Remember what you wrote in your application
- Give all the panel equal attention
- Help them give a good interview
- The more you answer, the less they ask
- Have a point of view about their business
- Make your experience sound useful
- Only talk about interests that are actually interesting

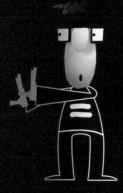

# New Arrival

Landing safely in a new job

- Get to know reception
- Explore the entire site
- Check you get what was promised
- Make friends with the office manager
- Say hello to the big boss
- Learn names fast
- Insist on the right kit from day one
- Assume everything is different
- Keep your ears, eyes and mind open
- Don't agree to anything in the first week

# Your Way

## How to start your own business

- Do something you're interested in
- Research your market and competitors
- Really understand what customers want
- Be clear how much money you can afford to lose
- Run the numbers again and again
- Prepare for things to take longer and cost more
- Pick your partners extremely carefully
- Try to start with one good customer
- Over-deliver to get yourself started
- Be a pleasure to do business with

**Guy Browning** is Managing Director of Smokehouse, an innovation consultancy. He has been a copywriter at DMB&B, Creative Director of the Added Value Company and a columnist for the *Guardian*, *People Management* and *Management Today*. He is a bestselling author and regular broadcaster on the BBC.

www.smokehouse.co.uk

**Janet Brown** studied graphic design at Camberwell College of Arts. She has worked at several top London agencies and is also a fine art illustrator. She is currently Design Director at Hog Design.

www.hogdesign.co.uk

Come and see the App!

www.skill-pill.com/guru

www.thepocketguru.co.uk